A BEACON  BIOGRAPHY

MEGAN RAPINOE

John Bankston

PURPLE TOAD
PUBLISHING

PURPLE TOAD
PUBLISHING

Printing   1   2   3   4   5   6   7   8   9

A Beacon Biography

Alexandria Ocasio-Cortez
Angelina Jolie
Anthony Davis
Ben Simmons
Big Time Rush
Bill Nye
Brie Larson
Bryce Harper
Cam Newton
Carly Rae Jepsen
Carson Wentz
Chadwick Boseman
Daisy Ridley
Drake
Ed Sheeran

Ellen DeGeneres
Elon Musk
Ezekiel Elliott
Gal Gadot
Harry Styles of One Direction
Jennifer Lawrence
Joel Embiid
John Boyega
Keanu Reeves
Kevin Durant
Lorde
Malala
Markus "Notch" Persson,
    Creator of Minecraft
Megan Rapinoe

Meghan Markle
Michelle Obama
Millie Bobby Brown
Misty Copeland
Mo'ne Davis
Muhammad Ali
Neil deGrasse Tyson
Oprah Winfrey
Peyton Manning
Robert Griffin III (RG3)
Scarlett Johansson
Stephen Colbert
Stephen Curry
Tom Holland
Zendaya

Library of Congress Cataloging-in-Publication Data
Bankston, John.
   Megan Rapinoe / Written by: John Bankston
      p.cm.
Includes bibliographic references, glossary, and index.
ISBN 978-1-62469-525-4
1. Megan Rapinoe, 1992- —Juvenile literature. 2. Women soccer players—United States—Biography—Juvenile literature. 3. Soccer players—United States—Biography—Juvenile literature. Series: I. A Beacon Biography.

 GV942.7. B36 2020
 796.334092 2

                                          Library of Congress Control Number 2019949380

eBook ISBN: 9781624695247

ABOUT THE AUTHOR: John Bankston is the author of over 150 books for young readers, including biographies of Kevin Durant, Venus Williams, and Abby Wambach. He has also written books about Major League Soccer teams including the Portland Timbers and the Chicago Fire SC. He lives in Miami Beach, Florida, with his ChiJack, Astronaut.

PUBLISHER'S NOTE: This story has not been authorized or endorsed by Megan Rapinoe.

CONTENTS

Megan Rapinoe celebrates her team's overtime victory over Brazil during the 2011 Women's World Cup.

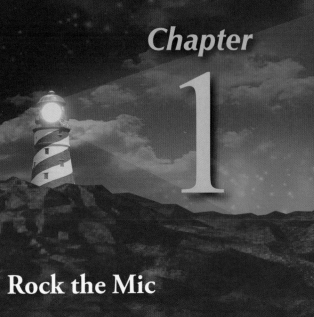

Chapter 1

Rock the Mic

Megan Rapinoe had just scored. It was the July 4th weekend and the 2011 Women's World Cup was under way. Her goal against Colombia would allow the U.S. to advance.

Around her, teammates raised their arms and cheered. Racing across the field, she retrieved a microphone. Picking it up, she tapped it to make sure it was on. Then she began to sing. Belting out the classic Bruce Springsteen song "Born in the U.S.A.," Rapinoe introduced herself to the world.[1]

Rapinoe is a midfielder. A soccer team's eleven players have specific roles. Goalies and defenders protect their team's goal. Forwards try to score goals. Midfielders are different. Lining up in the middle of the field, these players defend their own goal and also try to score. They have the ball more often than other players. Team captains are usually midfielders. David Beckham, one of the most famous soccer players in the world, was a midfielder. The position requires speed and stamina. Rapinoe had both. She also had a great sense of humor.

Abby Wambach inspired Megan both on and off the field.

In the 2011 Women's World Cup, team captain Abby Wambach was better known. And when the match began, Rapinoe wasn't racing across the field. She was riding the bench.

"I was surprised," she later admitted. "I have to be honest, I thought I had played well enough to be in the starting lineup. . . . I wanted to go out there and do my best to earn my spot back."[2]

It wasn't easy. Starting players remain in the game longer. Every team gets three substitute players. When a player is subbed out, she can't return to the field. Because of this, coaches are reluctant to bench their starters.

Playing against Brazil, the U.S. team endured brutal heat and a very long match. Most soccer games last 90 minutes. With the game tied, it went into overtime.

"We had just run ourselves ragged for 122 minutes. . . . Brazil, our opponents, were like the perfect sports movie villains," Rapinoe remembered. "After they took the lead in extra time, they [did] everything they could to waste time." By then, she was on the field. The game was almost over. The U.S. team was about to lose in the quarterfinals—the earliest World Cup exit in team history. [3]

Then defender Ali Krieger raced up the field. "All we had to do was go 100 yards and score without Brazil winning possession—the soccer equivalent of [football's] Hail Mary. No big deal, right?"[4]

Ali passed the ball to midfielder Carli Lloyd, who was swarmed by Brazil's defenders. Lloyd "turned her hips and dinked a pass" to Rapinoe. "I saw a blur of four yellow jerseys and a green one (not my teammate—their goalkeeper)." She couldn't see Wambach. But she knew where she would be. "I had to hit it with my left foot . . . I'm not naturally left-footed and usually I don't have as much power as I do with my right. So I hit it pretty much as hard as I could."[5]

"I was like, 'No, she's crushed it, just killed it,'" Wambach remembers. "I'm just standing there thinking, 'Get over [the goalie's] hands, over her head, and I've got a bead on the ball.' It comes over her hand, and I'm just thinking, 'Please, don't miss. This would be the most epic failure to have a wide-open goal and miss.' So I jump and connect with it and hit it, rather than letting the ball hit me."[6]

Whether on the field or watching from the sidelines, Rapinoe always supports her team.

Rapinoe remembers what happened next. "A second later, I saw the net shake. Then the stadium shook. It was absolute pandemonium."[7]

The header was the latest goal in World Cup history, for either men or women. With the score tied, a penalty kick shootout ended with the U.S. victorious. The team reached the finals, tying Japan before losing in penalty kicks. Despite the great shot, Rapinoe wasn't a starter until that last game.

Her twin sister, Rachael, was in London, watching the game on TV. "Watching Megan cross the ball and Abby heading it in the back of the net was one of the most magical soccer moments I have ever witnessed. . . . I have never been more proud of my sister."

For Megan Rapinoe, the path to World Cup stardom began in a struggling California town where she was taught by a patient older brother.[8]

Chapter 2

Early Talent

Megan Rapinoe can't remember when she wasn't playing soccer. Her older brother Brian would set up cones and she'd dribble the ball around them. Sometimes she'd use the inside of her foot. Then she'd focus on using the outside of her foot. She and her twin sister practiced until the sun set and her mother whistled for them to come inside. Megan was four years old.

"And it wasn't like he drilled them. He let them do it their own way," her mother, Denise, explained. "It was just the cutest thing, and we remember it so clearly."[1]

Megan and Rachael were born on July 5, 1985. Megan was the youngest of six, arriving just a few minutes after her twin. Their father, Jim, owned a construction company. Their mother, Denise, worked as a waitress at Jack's Grill. The family lived in Redding, California—some 250 miles north of San Francisco. The town of 90,000 seemed a world away from the coastal city.

"I feel like Redding is kind of this underdog, hardworking, blue-collar, is-what-it-is kind of town, and I try to take that with me," Rapinoe later explained. "I never want to just say, 'Oh, I'm from

California.' I'm not from California. I'm from Redding. For me, that means something."[2]

Growing up, Megan and her sister had one goal: to play sports as well as Brian. Sometimes they'd team up against him in a pickup game of basketball. Other times they'd work on soccer skills. "I worshipped him," Megan admits. "He played left wing, so I played left wing. He wore No. 7; I wore No. 7. He got a bowl cut, so I did too."[3]

When Megan entered Junction Elementary, she hoped to follow his path. She soon proved how well her brother had taught her. Long before Principal Jim Boesiger met Megan, he had heard about her. Lower-grade teachers described her as a "phenomenal athlete." Boesiger was stunned when Megan's seventh-grade soccer team easily beat the eighth graders.[4]

By the time she had graduated from eighth grade, Megan had been named Athlete of the Year. She broke the school record for the shuttle run physical fitness test. And she was making a name for herself away from sports. Her father doesn't remember exactly what Megan was talking about when she first spoke during a Junction Middle School Assembly. But he does remember thinking, "Who is this girl? Megan gets up and speaks as if she had been doing it her whole life."[5]

At Foothill High School, Megan played for the basketball team for three years. She was on the track team for two. She also got good grades, making the honor roll every semester. But she didn't play soccer at Foothill. She worried that top college programs wouldn't send recruiters there. Instead, she and Rachael played in Elk Grove, near Sacramento. Their parents had to drive 300 miles round-trip, four days a week. The twins played for Elk Grove Pride (the youth League) before joining Elk Grove United in the Women's Professional Soccer League. Pride coach Danny Cruz said that Megan "had it in her from the

Playing college soccer for the University of Portland Pilots, Megan displayed the same intensity that would make her a star.

beginning, she just needed a road map. I knew that she had the potential just by watching her play. I thought if I could just guide her and put her in the right spots, that her work was going to get her where she was going to go."[6]

The twins played for the professional United from 2002 to 2005. The strategy worked. When she graduated high school in 2003, Megan was offered a full scholarship to the University of Portland. There she would play for the school's champion soccer team, the Pilots. Megan was leaving her home, and leaving her family—but she wouldn't be alone. Rachael had earned a scholarship to play for the Pilots too!

Standing tall: Megan refuses to be intimidated on the field or off it.

Chapter 3

Choices

Every year, teens from all over the world leave their hometowns for college. Some travel thousands of miles. They seek new experiences and opportunities. Megan Rapinoe wanted those as well, but she had a more emotional reason for leaving.

When she was seven, she realized her older brother had started smoking marijuana. He was 12. She asked him why he did it, but Brian wasn't sure. "Right from the start, I was hooked," he says. "One drug always led to the next." Three years later, Brian was arrested for bringing meth to school. Their parents explained to Megan and Rachael that their brother would be going to juvenile detention. That was the beginning of hard times for Brian. For the next 20 years, he would be in and out of prison.[1]

For Megan and Rachael, leaving Redding meant leaving behind their brother's drug use and the people it had attracted. It was one reason they played in Elk Grove. It was also why they chose to leave the Central Valley for the Pacific Northwest.

Megan's college soccer career was delayed while she played for the U.S. in the 2004 Under-19 Women's World Championship. She helped the team reach third place.

Despite the delay, Megan had an amazing first season with the Pilots. The team was undefeated in 2005 and reached the Women's Soccer Championship. They won the College Cup final against UCLA 4-0. For her first year at Portland, she scored 15 goals (seven of them game-winning).

Instead of enjoying her summer break, Megan joined the U.S. women's national soccer team in 2006. She played matches against Ireland and scored her first goal with the team in a game against Taiwan. By then, she had returned to college play. As a sophomore, she was one of the country's top-ranked college midfielders. In her first 11 matches she scored 10 goals. Then during an October 2006 game against Washington State University, she was injured. She tore her ACL, an important ligament in the knee joint. The injury ended her season. The next year as a junior, she played just two games before injuring it again.

"I may have rushed back a little bit faster than I should have after the first ACL," she later admitted. "Not to say that was the reason that

Megan has torn her ACL knee ligament not once but twice, interrupting her college career.

Rapinoe turned pro in 2009 and was chosen to play in the WPS All Star Match.

it happened again, but the second one humbled me a bit in a lot of ways. I took my time and really allowed my body to heal and be as strong as possible."[2]

In 2008, she made up for lost time. As a senior she started all 22 games with the Pilots, helping them win 20 of them. She played in just 60 college games. Although these amounted to less than three seasons, she made 30 goals and 28 assists. She was ranked as the tenth best female soccer player in University of Portland history. In 2009, Megan followed the path set by many top college athletes. She turned pro. She was picked second in the Women's Professional Soccer (WPS) draft.

Unfortunately, women playing in the WPS earn far less than men playing in Major League Soccer (MLS). MLS players often earn hundreds of thousands of dollars. The average WPS player makes about as much as a cashier or a restaurant server. The WPS struggled to attract fans. In just a few years, Megan played for the Philadelphia Independence and the magicJack teams. In 2012, the league folded. By then, Megan faced tough choices—both in her career and in her personal life.

During the 2012 Olympics, Megan helped Team USA win the gold in their victory over Japan.

Coming Out

Megan Rapinoe missed her shot at the 2008 Olympics. As the 2012 games approached, she felt ready. Her body was rested and healed. She'd played several seasons of pro soccer, including a two-game guest appearance in Australia with Sydney Football Club. Qualifying for the U.S. Olympic team also sparked a decision. She'd made 52 international appearances with the team. She saw herself as an ambassador. One week before the games began in London, she did an interview with *Out*. She told the magazine that she was gay.

Rachael Rapinoe remembers her sister was always quiet and a bit shy in middle school. Now she thinks she knows why. "Maybe part of the reason why she was quiet growing up was because she felt a little different," she explained. "She didn't quite feel comfortable in her skin. But once she realized who she was, and why she felt the way she felt . . . that's when she found strength in her voice."[1]

As a starter on the team, Megan quickly racked up goals. She admitted, "It seems like a weight off my shoulders, because I'm playing a lot better than I've ever played before. . . . There are not many athletes that are out, and that was something that I felt was important to me."[2]

She broke a record in a semifinal game, landing a Goal Olimpico in a semifinal match against Canada. A Goal Olimpico is a corner kick that goes into the net without being touched by another player. No one had ever achieved this at the Olympics. The U.S. team went on to win the gold medal.

Back home, she began playing with the Seattle Sounders Women. Her teammates included stars like goalkeeper Hope Solo and forward Alex Morgan. Although they were fifth in their division when she joined, the next year they vaulted to just behind the Pali Blues, who played in the Los Angeles beachside community of Pacific Palisades. The Sounders lost to the Blues in the Western Conference Finals.

In 2013, Rapinoe spent six months playing with the French team Olympique Lyonnais. Afterward, she went to the Seattle Reign FC. Before she joined the team as a forward, the Reign had lost nine out of ten games. Alongside Solo, Rapinoe helped them win the National Women's Soccer League regular season title.

Alex Morgan and Rapinoe's friendship began when they played together for the Seattle Sounders.

With an assist from Abby Wambach, President Barack Obama participates in a "selfie" with the U.S. Women's National Soccer Team after they won the 2015 FIFA Women's World Cup.

After spending much of the 2011 Women's World Cup on the bench, 2015 saw her as a starter. She even scored her team's first goal in a winning match against Australia. The U.S. would go on to win the World Cup, beating Japan 5-2.

As a star player, Megan Rapinoe earned more than most professional women soccer players. Yet it wasn't playing but sponsorships that put her in the ranks of millionaire athletes. In 2009, she was signed by Nike. She explained that the company made a huge difference in her life: "I kind of knew while I was in college that I could make a living playing soccer, but I didn't dream anything to the level of what I'm doing now. . . . For a female athlete it's not always that way. Female athletes in the United States are pretty lucky."[3]

In 2016, another Nike-sponsored athlete became one of the most controversial on the company's roster. It was a fight Megan didn't run from. She joined it.

Motivated by San Francisco 49ers quarterback Colin Kaepernick's protest, Megan stood with her hands behind her during the National Anthem.

Winning More than Games

In the United States, most sporting events begin with the national anthem. Players and spectators usually stand quietly, facing the American flag, with their right hand over their heart, until it is over. During a 2016 National Football League preseason game against the Green Bay Packers, San Francisco 49ers quarterback Colin Kaepernick did something different. He kneeled.

The simple gesture was his protest against police shootings of African Americans. He later explained that he would not honor the anthem nor "show pride in a flag for a country that oppresses black people and people of color. To me, this is bigger than football and it would be selfish on my part to look the other way."[1]

His action divided football fans in a nation that already seemed bitterly divided over the upcoming presidential election between Donald Trump and Hillary Clinton. Some took his gesture not as a protest against police brutality, but as against the United States military.

To Megan Rapinoe, protesting the unfair treatment of minorities made sense. She began kneeling before her own games. "To me, it's literally all the same, insofar as I want people to respect who I am, what

Although many players and fans supported Kaepernick's anthem protest, it had unfortunate consequences. Despite leading his team to the Super Bowl in 2013, he was unable to get a job playing pro football for years after the 2016 season.

I am—being gay, being a woman, being a professional athlete, whatever," she later explained. "That is the exact same thing as what Colin did."[2]

When U.S. Soccer began requiring their male and female athletes to stand during the anthem, Rapinoe did so but wouldn't sing or place her hand over her heart. Trump's victory in 2016 helped fuel extensive player protests during the next year's football season. Rapinoe believed the president was opposed to gay rights and equality.

In 2015, the U.S. Supreme Court ruled that the Constitution's Fourteenth Amendment requires all states to grant same-sex marriages. Soon after, Rapinoe and her girlfriend, singer Sera Cahoone, became engaged. The couple later broke up, and Rapinoe began dating Sue Bird, who played with the Women's National Basketball Association's Seattle Storm.

In 2018, Rapinoe and Bird shared the cover of *ESPN* magazine's Body Issue. "I think having a gay couple on [the cover], hopefully it just becomes the norm," Bird said. "You want it to not be an issue. You want it to just be, Oh, another couple is on there. You know, I think for us to be on it is the first step in that direction."[3]

In 2019, Rapinoe was once again a starter for the U.S. women's team. Yet winning their second World Cup in a row was not the only thing on players' minds. Just three months before their first match in France, they sued the United States Soccer Federation. They believed the Federation treated male and female athletes differently. They sued because male players were paid more, even though the women had won three of seven titles since the Women's World Cup began in 1991. The U.S. men's team did not qualify for the 2018 World Cup. The women's team also attracts more fans and sells out more stadiums than the men's team. Nike reported that in 2019, the U.S. women's home jersey was its top-selling soccer jersey for either men or women ever.[4]

Besides training and playing as hard as the men, the U.S. Women's National Soccer Team has won more games and sold more tickets. The women feel they deserve to be paid the same as the Men's National Team players.

Determined and ready for anything, Becky Sauerbrunn and Megan Rapinoe are trying to win more than just games.

"The bottom line is simple," defender Becky Sauerbrunn explained. "It is wrong for us to be paid and valued less for our work because of our gender." Rapinoe added that she thinks the lawsuit is important not only for the team but for "future teammates, fellow women athletes and women all around the world."[5]

When the team began playing in the World Cup in France, it sometimes seemed like no one wanted to talk about soccer. After Rapinoe said she wouldn't visit the White House, President Trump called her out on Twitter, saying she should WIN before she talks. Not long after Trump's tweet, Rapinoe scored both of the goals in the U.S. quarterfinal victory over France.

Yet in her hometown the celebrations were muted. Although California voters overwhelmingly supported Clinton, Trump received 64 percent of the vote in Shasta County, where Redding is located. Many Redding soccer fans supported her playing but not her politics. Her father was one of them. "I voted for Trump," Jim Rapinoe explained. Still, he wished the President would stay off Twitter. "The guy does more harm than good. This is all you have to do today? Just get on Megan on a comment she made from a while ago?"[6]

Crystal Dunn and Megan Rapinoe celebrate a goal against England.

The team also faced criticism for celebrating too much during their 13-0 win over Thailand. In response, players celebrated with a quiet "golf clap" after Carli Lloyd scored a goal against France. When they played England, new World Cup player Alex Morgan pretended to sip from a teacup after scoring. Rapinoe defended their celebrations.

"We're at the World Cup," she pointed out. "What do you want us to do? This is the biggest stage, the biggest moment. . . . We work hard. We like to play hard."[7]

The final game against the Netherlands represented the first time both Women's World Cup teams had female head coaches, with the U.S.'s Jill Ellis and the Netherlandss' Sarina Wiegman. Rapinoe had sat out the game against England, nursing an injured hamstring. Just one hour into the game against the Netherlands, Rapinoe scored with a penalty kick. The goal made her the oldest woman to score in a Women's World Cup final. Eight minutes later, Rose Lavelle scored—sending the U.S. team to a 2-0 victory. It was the team's fourth World Cup and their second in a row. When Rapinoe left the field, fans stood up and cheered.

In 2020, the U.S. Women's National Soccer Team (USWNT) and the U.S. Soccer Federation (USSF) would meet in federal court. A judge would decide if the women should be paid what they feel they are worth. Meanwhile, ESPN is again airing National Women's Soccer League games. Rapinoe is one of 15 USWNT players in the league.

In 2020, Rapinoe would publish books about social justice and her journey. One is for adults, the other for younger readers. Some of what she has written reflects the advice she gave to Junction students: "Every one of you has something special to offer," she said. "And if you believe in yourself, it will give you special power to achieve your goals. Don't be afraid. Grab hold of life and make it what you want it to be. And never quit believing in yourself, no matter what happens."[8]

Rapinoe's belief in herself and willingness to take risks are part of why she is celebrated for more than just her soccer ability. It is also why she will continue to be well known long after she hangs up her cleats for good.

2019	Women's World Cup Golden Boot
2015	National Women's Soccer League Player of the Week (shared with others)
	Outstanding Team Award, ESPN
2014	Inducted into Shasta County Sports Hall of Fame
2013	Board of Directors Award from the Los Angeles Gay and Lesbian Center
2012	Harry Glickman Professional Female Athlete of the Year
2005	Soccer Times National Freshman of the Year
	NSCAA First Team All-American
	Soccer Buzz and Soccer America First Team Freshman All-American
	Soccer Buzz West Region Freshman of the Year
	West Coast Conference Freshman of the Year
2004	Parade All-American
	National Soccer Coaches Association of America (NSCAA) All-American
2003	Parade All-American

CHRONOLOGY

1985	Megan Anna Rapinoe and twin sister Rachael are born on July 5 to Jim and Denise Rapinoe. They live in Redding, California.
1989	Megan's brother Brian begins teaching her how to play soccer.
1991	Megan plays soccer and attends Junction Elementary and Junction Middle School.
2002—2005	She plays club soccer with Elk Grove United, which is part of the Women's Premiere Soccer League.
2003	Megan graduates from Foothill High School and enters the University of Portland.
2004	She competes in the Under-19 Women's World Championship with the U.S. team, placing third.
2005	Megan plays her first season as a Pilot with the University of Portland.
2006	She joins the United States women's national soccer team.
2008	She graduates from the University of Portland with a degree in sociology.
2009	Megan is the number two pick in the Women's Professional Soccer (WPS) draft. She plays for the Chicago Red Stars.
2011	Rapinoe assists Abby Wambach during the Women's World Cup match against Brazil with a goal in the 122nd minute of play.
2012	In a magazine interview, Megan comes out as gay. She plays with the U.S. team at the London Olympics, where they win gold.
2015	She becomes engaged to singer Sera Cahoone. They later split.
2018	Megan appears alongside Sue Bird as the first same-sex couple on the cover of ESPN magazine's Body Issue.
2019	She is the first openly gay woman to pose for *Sports Illustrated*'s swimsuit issue. She helps the U.S. women's national soccer team win their fourth World Cup.
2020	Her books on social justice—one for adults and one for middle readers—are published.

Chapter 1. Rock the Mic

1. "Megan Rapinoe Scores for Team USA and Sings 'Born in the USA.' " *YouTube*, July 4, 2011. https://www.youtube.com/watch?v=oepayP5R33g
2. Goldberg, Jamie. "Megan Rapinoe Overcomes Setbacks to Shine in First World Cup." *The Oregonian*, July 19, 2011. https://www.oregonlive.com/fifa-world-cup/2011/07/megan_rapinoe_overcomes_setbac.html
3. Rapinoe, Megan. "The Cross." *Players Tribune*, December 16, 2014. https://www.theplayerstribune.com/en-us/articles/the-cross
4. Ibid.
5. Ibid.
6. Wahl, Grant. "The 10 Most Significant Goals In U.S. Soccer History: Abby Wambach, 2011." *Sports Illustrated*, https://www.si.com/longform/soccer-goals/goal9.html
7. Rapinoe.
8. Goldberg.

Chapter 2. Early Talent

1. Oxenham, Gwendolyn. "Why Megan Rapinoe's Brother Brian Is Her Greatest Heartbreak, and Hope." *ESPN*, July 7, 2019. https://www.espn.com/soccer/fifa-womens-world-cup/story/3878587/why-megan-rapinoes-brother-brian-is-her-greatest-heartbreakand-hope
2. Almond, Elliot. "Women's World Cup: Hometown Star Stirs Mixed Feelings in California's Trump Country." *Mercury News*, July 6, 2019. https://www.mercurynews.com/2019/07/06/womens-world-cup-hometown-star-out-of-step-in-californias-trump-country/
3. Oxenham.
4. "Megan Rapinoe Urges Junction Students to Follow Their Dreams." *East Valley Times*, September 15, 2011. https://evalleytimes.com/news/megan-rapinoe-urges-junction-students-to-follow-their-dreams/
5. Almond.
6. Breton, Marcos. "Megan Rapinoe Took Her First Steps Toward Soccer Stardom in Elk Grove." *The Sacramento Bee*, July 9, 2019. https://www.sacbee.com/news/local/article232410607.html

Chapter 3. Choices

1. Oxenham, Gwendolyn. "Why Megan Rapinoe's Brother Brian Is Her Greatest Heartbreak, and Hope." *ESPN*, July 7, 2019. https://www.espn.com/soccer/fifa-womens-world-cup/story/3878587/why-megan-rapinoes-brother-brian-is-her-greatest-heartbreakand-hope
2. Klemko, Robert. "Rapinoe Enters Games with Healthy Outlook." *USA Today*, July 10, 2012, p. 03C.

Chapter 4. Coming Out

1. Bushnell, Henry. "Megan Rapinoe Is a 'Walking Protest.' " *Yahoo Sports*, May 13, 2019. https://sports.yahoo.com/megan-rapinoe-is-a-walking-protest-162416461.html
2. "Rapinoe Relaxed, Proud after 'Coming Out' Party." *New York Post*, August 9, 2012, p. 59.
3. Klemko, Robert. "Rapinoe Enters Games with Healthy Outlook." *USA Today*, July 10, 2012, p. 03C.

Chapter 5. Winning More than Games

1. McKirdy, Euan. "NFL Star Colin Kaepernick Sits in Protest during National Anthem." *CNN*, August 28, 2016.
2. Longman, Jere. "An Athlete and Advocate Who Refuses to Yield." *New York Times*, June 28, 2019, p. B7(L).
3. Flynn, Meagan. "Seattle Sports Stars Sue Bird and Megan Rapinoe Are First Same-Sex Couple on Cover of *ESPN* Body Issue." *Washington Post*, June 26, 2018.
4. Bachman, Rachel, and Joshua Robinson. "U.S. Women Turn Up the Noise." *The Wall Street Journal*, July 6–7, 2019.
5. Goodman, Lizzy. "The Grass Ceiling." *The New York Times Magazine*, June 16, 2019, p. 40(L).
6. Almond, Elliot. "Women's World Cup: Hometown Star Stirs Mixed Feelings in California's Trump Country." *Mercury News*, July 6, 2019. https://www.mercurynews.com/2019/07/06/womens-world-cup-hometown-star-out-of-step-in-californias-trump-country/
7. Bachman and Robinson.
8. "Megan Rapinoe Urges Junction Students to Follow Their Dreams." *East Valley Times*, September 15, 2011. https://evalleytimes.com/news/megan-rapinoe-urges-junction-students-to-follow-their-dreams/

Books
Killion, Ann. *Champions of Women's Soccer*. New York: Philomel Books, 2018.

Nagelhout, Ryan. *Soccer: Who Does What?* New York: Gareth Stevens Publishing, 2018.

Peterson, Megan Cooley. *Stars of Women's Soccer*. Mankato, Minnesota: Black Rabbit Books, 2018.

Skinner, J. E. *U.S. Women's National Soccer Team*. Ann Arbor, Michigan: Cherry Lake, 2019.

On the Internet
Learn How to Play Soccer:

    https://www.ducksters.com/sports/soccer.php

Learn about Megan:

    https://www.ussoccer.com/players/r/megan-rapinoe

See the Play from Chapter One: "Megan Rapinoe Scores for Team USA and Sings 'Born in the USA,' " YouTube, July 4, 2011.

    https://www.youtube.com/watch?v=oepayP5R33g

Works Consulted
Almond, Elliot. "Women's World Cup: Hometown Star Stirs Mixed Feelings in California's Trump Country." *Mercury News*, July 6, 2019. https://www.mercurynews.com/2019/07/06/womens-world-cup-hometown-star-out-of-step-in-californias-trump-country/

Bachman, Rachel, and Joshua Robinson. "U.S. Women Turn Up the Noise." *The Wall Street Journal*, July 6–7, 2019.

Bell, Brian C. "Megan Rapinoe Leads U.S. to 2019 Women's World Cup Title." *Outsports*, July 7, 2019. https://www.outsports.com/2019/7/7/20685241/soccer-uswnt-usa-world-cup-megan-rapinoe-women-netherlands

Bieler, Des. "USWNT's Megan Rapinoe Becomes First Openly Gay Woman to Pose for *SI* Swimsuit Issue." *Washington Post*, May 9, 2019.

——. "WNBA Star Sue Bird Comes Out as Gay, Says She's Dating USWNT's Megan Rapinoe." *Washington Post*, July 20, 2017.

Breton, Marcos. "Megan Rapinoe Took Her First Steps Toward Soccer Stardom in Elk Grove." *The Sacramento Bee*, July 9, 2019. https://www.sacbee.com/news/local/article232410607.html

Bushnell, Henry. "Megan Rapinoe Is a 'Walking Protest.' " *Yahoo Sports*, May 13, 2019. https://sports.yahoo.com/megan-rapinoe-is-a-walking-protest-162416461.html

Deahl, Rachel. "Megan Rapinoe Signs with Penguin for Adult, MG Books." *Publisher's Weekly*, July 25, 2019. https://www.publishersweekly.com/pw/by-topic/industry-news/book-deals/article/80761-rapinoe-signs-with-penguin-for-adult-mg-titles.html

Flynn, Meagan. "Seattle Sports Stars Sue Bird and Megan Rapinoe Are First Same-Sex Couple on Cover of *ESPN* Body Issue." *Washington Post*, June 26, 2018.

Goff, Steven, and Emily Giambalvo. "U.S. Wins World Cup with a Final Four-Star Performance." *Washington Post*, July 7, 2019. https://www.washingtonpost.com/sports/2019/07/07/uswnt-netherlands-world-cup-final/?utm_term=.2a429a714f6b

Goldberg, Jamie. "Megan Rapinoe Overcomes Setbacks to Shine in First World Cup." *The Oregonian*, July 19, 2011. https://www.oregonlive.com/fifa-world-cup/2011/07/megan_rapinoe_overcomes_setbac.html

Goodman, Lizzy. "The Grass Ceiling." *The New York Times Magazine*, June 16, 2019, p. 40(L). https://longform.org/posts/the-grass-ceiling

Hutchins, Andy. "Video: USWNT's Megan Rapinoe Does Best Bruce Springsteen Impression in Goal Celebration." *SB Nation*, July 2, 2011. https://www.sbnation.com/soccer/2011/7/2/2256131/megan-rapinoe-bruce-springsteen-impression-goal-celebration-video

Klemko, Robert. "Rapinoe Enters Games with Healthy Outlook." *USA Today*, July 10, 2012, p. 03C.

Longman, Jere. "An Athlete and Advocate Who Refuses to Yield." *The New York Times*, June 28, 2019, p. B7(L).

McKirdy, Euan. "NFL Star Colin Kaepernick Sits in Protest during National Anthem." *CNN*, August 28, 2016. https://www.cnn.com/2016/08/28/sport/nfl-colin-kaepernick-protest-sit-down-national-anthem/index.html

"Megan Rapinoe Scores for Team USA and Sings 'Born in the USA,'" *YouTube*, July 4, 2011. https://www.youtube.com/watch?v=oepayP5R33g

"Megan Rapinoe Urges Junction Students to Follow Their Dreams." *East Valley Times*, September 15, 2011. https://evalleytimes.com/news/megan-rapinoe-urges-junction-students-to-follow-their-dreams/

Oxenham, Gwendolyn. "Why Megan Rapinoe's Brother Brian Is Her Greatest Heartbreak, and Hope." *ESPN*, July 7, 2019. https://www.espn.com/soccer/fifa-womens-world-cup/story/3878587/why-megan-rapinoes-brother-brian-is-her-greatest-heartbreakand-hope

Rapinoe, Megan. "The Cross." *Players Tribune*, December 16, 2014. https://www.theplayerstribune.com/en-us/articles/the-cross

"Rapinoe Is Named to U.S. Women's Soccer Team." *The New York Times*, July 13, 2016, p. B14(L).

"Rapinoe Relaxed, Proud after 'Coming Out' Party." *The New York Post*, August 9, 2012, p. 59.

"Singer Sera Cahoone Engaged to Soccer Star Megan Rapinoe." *World Entertainment News Network*, August 7, 2015.

Wahl, Grant. "The 10 Most Significant Goals In U.S. Soccer History: Abby Wambach, 2011." *Sports Illustrated*, https://www.si.com/longform/soccer-goals/goal9.html

Wulfhart, Nell McShane. "What This Star of Soccer Packs For the Road." *New York Times*, June 23, 2019, p. 2(L).

GLOSSARY

controversial (kahn-truh-VER-shul)—Argued about.

ligament (LIG-ah-ment)—Tissue that connects bones to other bones.

mediate (meed-EE-ate)—Discussion used to settle lawsuits, usually before a judge.

marijuana (mayr-ih-WAH-nah)—A type of plant that is used as a medicine or drug.

meth (METH)—A chemical that is used as a drug.

minority (meh-NAR-ih-tee)—A smaller part of a group.

pandemonium (pan-deh-MOH-nee-um)—A very loud and confused situation, such as a panicked crowd.

professional (proh-FEH-shuh-nul)—A person who is paid to do a job.

qualify (KWAL-ih-fy)—Able to compete in a tournament after fulfilling certain requirements.

quarterfinal (kwar-ter-FY-nul)—A competition among the top 8 teams in a league that determines which teams will play in the championship.

recruiter (re-KROOT-er)—Scouts who find talented athletes and convince them to play for a college or pro team.

PHOTO CREDITS: Cover, pp. 1, 4, 7, 11, 12, 18, 20, 23, 24, 25—Jamie Smed; p. 6—Beefalo; p. 8—Ron Reiring; pp. 14, 16—Joel Solomon; p. 15—John Maxmena; p. 19—The White House; p. 22—Mike Morbeck; p. 27—Lorie Shaull. Every measure has been taken to find all copyright holders of material used in this book. In the event any mistakes or omissions have occurred,, attempts to correct them will be made in future editions of the book.